AF490590

A

Poet's

Grief

By

Karnika Moudgil

"To the person in my head, thank you for believing in me and continuing to even when no one did"

A Letter From The Poet

The 1st of January 2024, is when I challenged myself to write a book of poems and publish it before the year ends. Five months later, I now have about a hundred poems and a somewhat experienced poet. I've always been a writer, but a poet? Not so much. However, these past five months have made poetry, my escape from reality. There have been ups and downs through this journey, and this book was with me for all of it. It's seen days where I wrote five poems a day, and its seen times I didn't write for weeks on end. It's seen me love a poem one day, only to cringe at it the next and delete it. All in all, it's been my best friend and while I don't want to let go, its now time for me to pass it on to you, beloved reader. I hope if not anything, by the end of this book at least one of these poems, make you fall in love with poetry, awakens the poet in you and makes you want to pour your thoughts onto paper. I hope this book means to you, as much as it did to me. I crave, that for you this book becomes the one you read again, simply for comfort when you feel like the world just doesn't understand. With that dear reader, I bid a fond farewell and leave you with a fragment of myself in the form of these poems.

Pensively yours,
Karnika Moudgil

Contents

1. The Air is Thick, I Cannot Breathe

The air is thick, I cannot breathe
This city, this house, I once called home, is now nothing but
a broken mould

 There's nothing left for me to give, this place slowly took
away, everything I once was and everything I could've been.
It's best for me, father, that I must leave
For, the air is thick, I cannot breathe

All my emotions finished flowing,
I feel hollowed, I feel numb
Forgive me mother, for I made you weep,
But, there's nothing left for me in this house, this town, this
busy street.
The air is thick, dear lord, I cannot breathe.

2. A Great Escape

A great escape, from all I've ever known,
 happiness in this place is nothing but a loan
which must be paid back in due time,
doubled back with interest, all right

A great escape is what I seek, go ahead call me weak,
but I shall not bow down like those before me.
I shall run off, break free, but I shall not bow down
like those before me

To run with the wind, sail with the sea,
what a marvellous life it shall be,
To break the cycle and complete
my life's goal of symphony
After all, a great escape is all I need,
to run off away from my misery

3. The Moon Has Insecurities Too

You tell me I look like the moon,
and say things that would make every girl
swoon but all I see are the moon's craters,
 the darkness beneath

After all, the moon has insecurities too
darker than the sun, the stars aglow,
forgetting its purities, what's hidden beneath,
the cool water ice nobody sees.

So maybe then, it's not so bad
When you tell me I look like the moon
Maybe, I should be glad that you love me not just on the
surface
But, my craters and darkness all of my view
After all, the moon has insecurities too

4. The 'Best' Friend

I'm never the 'best' friend,
Never the one someone tells secrets first to
I'm the friend who gets pity invites, who gets told
they can't come by people trying to be nice

I'm never the first, always the second
And every second I live, I must be felt like it
And never feel bad, not one bit
I never know the school gossip,
The amount I speak, I could clock it
5 minutes, 2, 10 on good days
What I do the rest of the time, it's all a haze

But after all I guess that's okay,
Knowing, all my 'friends' are fake

5. The Perfect Murder

The perfect murder,
I have it all planned to sit alone,
and slice my own hand

To take me to a better world, up in the clouds,
I've been a good man
Let me rest, in peace alas,
if all goes according to plan

Let me bleed, through my clothes
Let the crimson cleanse my soul,
Pass my suffering on to others,
Why? The cycle must continue after all
For the perfect murder I have it all planned,
walk out unscathed, tired of god's plan

6. A Girl Who Never Speaks

The quiet girl who never speaks,
Has a thousand secrets hidden beneath,
her glasses and long brown hair

She never responds, only stares
The stare that says 'leave me alone'
rumour says, her heart's made of stone
Her still waters run quite deep,
Deeper than the trenches, deeper than the sea

For a flicker, you can see in her eyes,
 loneliness and longing
Wishing for company, but alas
that is simply not possible
For, what the class needs, is a lonely girl in the back
with a book to read

7. Academic Rivals

They're academic rivals,
they hate each other,
constantly the ones trying to be better

Except everyone else, can see they're smitten,
the constant stolen glances, the eyes,
they do secret dances

They hide behind the curtain of hate,
while love does it's play
If they were in a book they'd have confessed by now,
instead of hiding it fear bound

If only they were fictional,
it wouldn't be such a tragedy,
 but they're real,
and nothing in the real world is ever ecstasy

So they pretend,
and pretend they do till their days end
Because, They're academic rivals,
they have to hate each other of course
They have to, right?

8. I'm Starting To Forget Your Voice

I'm starting to forget your voice
Believe me I wouldn't, if I had a choice
The thought of it, the thought of never seeing you again,
never holding you close

Those brown eyes and that long beautiful nose
I'm starting to forget your voice, the conversations we had
While that breaks me to the core,
You were and are the one I'll forever love most

If I could go back in time, I would
Not to change a thing, just hear your words,
one last time to memorise it all
Your scent, your gait, everything in between
For one last time, I wish for you to be seen

Grandmother, oh sweet
 if I had a choice,
I'd never let you go without me
Now, I'm starting to forget your voice

9. As Simple As a Poem

If only life were as simple as a poem
Life would be nothing but a walk of serenity,
Loved by the writer, surrounded by words

It would be as simple as finding a clever rhyme
We'd have all day, all it's time
Poetic devices, we'd use as vices
Metaphors, and personify book characters

If only life were as simple as a poem,
It would be short, and sweet
Each word dancing to its own beat
Repeat it all at the day's dawn,
The poem that we had begun

If only life were as simple as a poem

10. Fifty More Years

If we could live fifty more years,
Maybe we'd have enough time, to get over those fears

Those irrational, uncontrollable,
Fears of the heart
It's inescapable breaking, oh here come the tears

If only we could live fifty more years, we'd make it, see our
sons and daughters age, like fine wine locked away

It's scary to think how one day, we shall no longer live, just
simply vanish into thin air
The tragic, inevitable death, we'd embrace it if we had more
time

If only we could live fifty more years, alas we can't our end is
near
How wonderful could it have been?
If only we could live fifty more years

11. The Favourite Subject

I'm not the one who gets straight As
No matter how much I study nothing stays,
 in this ignorant brain of mine,

It's be so easy, if the test was about you, and your ways
The way you play with that bracelet on your wrist,
The way playfully, your eyes you twist

If only this was taught in school,
I'd ace my tests, if only that was the rule
After all, your what I think about,
the one who clouds my thoughts

If only you were a subject to study,
you'd be my favourite one,
making me melt like putty

12. The Person I Used To Be

I miss the person I was before,
I miss my happiness, my warmth
How I found myself enough,
even when the times got tough

For the person I am now,
makes me ashamed,
so weak, broken at the brain
I miss the person,
I was before, I fell down this deep rabbit hole

I miss being the one who'd never disappoint
I'll forever feel the void,
Of being the person I was before,
when I was once filled with hope

13. Lasts Forever

Nothing good, lasts forever
Time passes and flowers wither
Like feelings, disappearing
as if they weren't there

Humans wither into dust,
Iron changes into rust,
nothing can stop the inevitable change

For if something was good,
It wouldn't last anyway

14. Poor heartless One

You were heartless, with only a brain
With ice running through your veins,
Your bones are made of nothing but stones, for if you had a
heart
You wouldn't be alone,

You wouldn't roam the cold streets,
With a microscopic heart, incapable of love
Of your games, I've had enough

Emotions were never built for you,
Maybe someone out there is
But to me, you were and always will be
The Heartless one with ice running through his veins

15. The Villain

I'd like to be the villain not hero,
It's much more fun being the cause,
To end the world, with applause

I'd go down in the books of those,
Along the greatest of foes
Poison would be my favourite dish
Along with revenge, cold served of course

I'd rather be a villain,
who'd burn the world that did her wrong,
Than a lawful hero singing his song

16. The Oxygen I Need

For me, you are oxygen and water
Everything, one needs to survive
Things essential for life

I need you now and I'll need you forever
But to you, I am only unnecessary
All things secondary, is what I am to you

But I don't blame you, I'm not the conventional beautiful
I hated how I looked, all through out my lonely childhood
I could never understand why someone would love me,
like I love you

As Unfair as it might be,
I'm all right as long as I have you,
my oxygen to breathe
Even if it's only from afar,
I'm okay with that, happy in my heart

Because, for me you are the oxygen and water I need,
Your simple presence makes me relieved

17. When I Turn Eighteen

I wish for the day I turn eighteen
The day I go free, out in the world green
To make my own decisions, I'd love is what I thought

But now as each year goes, the date gets close
And I'm rather afraid of the thought
What if I make my life's worst mistake

What if I waste my young days? Being caged by my own mind
Regretting the things I didn't do right?

So I wish for the day I turn eighteen
To come and end this epiphany

18. Feel Alone

Don't you ever feel alone?
Like everything you've ever worked for is gone?
Everyone you've ever loved forgotten

Every thing you ever touched lost
All paths crossed, straightened
Cold, lonely and mistaken

That there were people who loved you,
They wanted to protect you
But now it all seems like a figment
Of your poor imagination

19. A Blood Red Rose

A rose, blood red,
So pure, so true
If only it was
I wish I knew

The rose you gave me pricked my skin,
While I admired its beauty, it killed me from within

I didn't know until it was too late
For the pain felt good
On that poor day,
I threw the rose away it withered
While my heart it stopped its flutter

20. I'm Toxic

I'm toxic, as red as a red flag can be
Left by many, who got tired of me
But what can I do?
No matter how hard I try,
they always find a reason

A reason to leave, break the thread that tied us together,
and roam free
I replied too late,
my replies were too short

Cut me some slack, I'm trying after all
I can't change in a second,
like the guys in your books do
I'm a human after all,
it'll take me some time,
but I'll change for you

21. Petrichor Smell

The clouds in the sky are gray
Dampening, and darkening my lonesome day

I sit on a bench and let the rain drench
Myself, take away all of my stress and my worries

I relax, as I hear the thunder,
My mother's assurance,
The lightning before it gives me peace

The petrichor smell, it breaths life into me
And gives me hope to a certain degree

22. Black Elixir

My coffee is dark, both bitter and sweet
I always have it from the Café from down the street
I sit in the exact same seat, give the waiter a gaze,

He knows what to bring me,
To take my pain away
Enough to last me through the day

I hold the warm cup in my hands tight,
like it's something I stole
I guzzle down the black elixir like it's water,
breathing life into my soul

Trying to forget about my life's impending goals,
Drinking them down, before the coffee gets cold

23. A Wish Upon The Stars And Comets

As soft as a pillow,
as light as a feather
Hold me close in this stormy weather

Wrap me in your arms
like I belong under your skin,
melting into you that's where I live

The comfort your touch provides me,
the mellowness in it
Soon, we'll build our kingdom, bit by bit
But for now, we stare at the sky
and make a wish on the stars and the comets

24. The Voice In My Head

I'm afraid I'll never be enough
Not for anyone else, just myself
Being out of touch, with reality

Making the one wrong decision,
Not doing what I love
I'm afraid I won't fill in the shoes of expectations
 Set by no one but myself

Setup by my own self, to fall in deep despair
I'm afraid I'll never be enough
I could and will never be for me,
For that little voice in my head tells me
 there's still so much I can be

25. I Feel You In My Room

I can feel your presence in my room,
For that fleeting moment,
 where out goes the gloom

The moment when for just a bare second,
The clouds move aside, letting the light in

For that one millisecond I feel your touch,
was it your soul or the tricks of my mind such,
 to try and make me feel your warmth?
For, there's nothing like it
The second passes, and the gloom comes back

Bringing me on to the dark track,
Sweeping dust into my brain,
Rather carefully with a broom,
I feel your presence in my room

26. My Sister's Keeper

I never say much,
But to my sisters I bare my soul
For I know, they'll see me,
Won't make me feel small

They'll give me advice on what they couldn't do, I should
I know in a heartbeat, they'll take a stand for me
Won't leave me, take my hand guide me for eternity

So when they just need someone to listen, I stay
And pay attention, to the way they talk
about their frustrations, the crushes they had
Smiling inside, being glad
making me their sister, a built in friend
For I know, I wont find one like them
even if I search till the earths end

27. A Letter For My Ace

It is sad how you shall never know,
how much I love you so
For I will never be able to say it to your face
Instead I seal it all up in a letter,
For you my ace,

I keep it locked away, never to be sent
For my feelings I would rather hide,
Than have them be broken by your non acceptance

It's obvious, how could anyone love someone like me?
I don't have what it takes, I can't handle it, I'm too weak
So I shall mourn this loss of what I shall never speak
Even if my feelings continue to grow so,
It is sad, how much
 I wish you knew, I loved you so

28. A Tattoo Of Your Face

I'll get a tattoo of your face,
It'll stay with me forever,
I won't let the ink fade away

If I could talk to the dead,
you'd be the first I'd walk to
Share everything since you've been gone

They think I've gone crazy,
But they won't get it anyway
They don't have what we have
They would've simply walked away
But for you, I'd stay
And stay I would, until the seasons change

29. My Therapist Says

My therapist says I've gone insane
 when I tell her about my pain,
It just won't go away,
I know it's all in my head,
 that's where it stays

I can't explain it but,
it brings me pain and pleasure in a way
I've lost my marbles, my sanity, all of it
But bit by bit, this pain encourages

Me to give it all up,
everything I've worked to towards,
everything I am
To pack it all away, and move to a strange land

Hearing this, my therapist says I've gone insane

30. I'm (not) an only child

I'm an only child,
 but it didn't used to be this away,
It wasn't until the older one,
packed his bags, moved apart

Leaving me to pick up the broken pieces,
 of what was left of my existence,
for the rest he took along with him
We never talk now, each on one's own way,
while I try to bend, learn to live this way

I won't admit it, never in a thousand days,
won't tell him I miss him, won't message or call,

but I'm an only child now,
and I'm certainly not okay...

31. We'll Meet Again

Someday we'll meet again,
Someday I'll relieve the pain
Someday, my efforts won't all go in vain

I remember the one conversation we had,
I remember how I laughed with you
Like with no one else I could the same
I'll ascertain why you left, we'll never be apart again

But for now I bid goodbye
Your in the sky, I'm on cold hard land,
someday we'll meet again

32. We Wouldn't Dare

Maybe I'm not fine,
You were meant to be mine
We both know it,
but we wouldn't dare

I miss your scent,
I miss your care
We belong, yes we do
But we wouldn't dare

As I leave I hoped maybe you'd stop me,
maybe you'd call me
Text me, something
What we had was nothing short of rare
We both know it, but we wouldn't dare

33. Soulmates By Choice

With you, I know I'll be fine
The only one who'd take my call
in the dead of night

We were family, by chance but
Became friends by choice
Born to fill each others voids

We're sisters by chance,
but each others confidants by choice
The only one I'd stand up to fight for,
even if my knees give out, my bones ignite

For we're family by chance,
But each others soulmates by choice

34. Easier Said Than Done

It's easier said than done,
To finish what I once begun
Not easy to see, my life's work
Undone

For accomplished I have none,
My family thinks right,
maybe I'm not meant for this,
maybe not quite

It's easier said than done,
But I'll still try,
Try I will while my bones cry
While they ache for me to stop,
My mind says no,
I have to show them,
I have to, for it will be easier said than done,
If the work is never begun

35. We Were Friends

I thought we were friends,
But you slowly stopped talking,
While with others you were laughing

I thought we'd be the kind of friends
 who stay friends till their end,
Ride or dies, but I guess you chose the death, of us
It's fair I guess maybe, it was time for us to end

I thought we were friends,
But I don't anymore,
for I watched you walk right out that door

36. Since We Were Small

I can tell them anything,
They'll listen, with me
I know they'd stand tall

At school, I had no friends,
but I was fine
Knowing those two special girls,
 those sisters of mine

Ones left,
ones right,
but I stand at the centre and hold them tight
And I know I'll never let them go,
for it's a sisters promise,
 for them I'd burn the world
and watch it fall

They're my big sisters,
 I've loved them for eternity,
since we were small

37. For Cocoa

If only dogs could live longer than us,
Then I wouldn't be afraid,
of watching you pass

I'd be the one to die,
with you by my side
For when humans weren't there for me,
you were with your paw on mine

If only dogs could live longer than us,
it'd be a better world,
maybe one happier than mine

38. Insecurities

Maybe if I was thinner,
I'd feel like a winner
No matter what I did,
I'd feel worth something

If I had a thigh gap,
A pretty face,
no ugly scabs of who I used to be
Then maybe, I'd feel like me

I wouldn't have to hide behind baggy clothes,
I wouldn't have to compensate with jokes

Maybe if I was thinner, I'd be accepted more,
but then would I miss who
I used to be, who I am now?

39. To My Dear Dead Grandmother

Even though I don't show it,
I hated god for it,
I want you back from a place
I know you can't return from

I miss your face, soft and warm
Your presence that made me calm
I know your better away from the suffering,

But letting you go, he's withering away
 till he slowly reaches the place you are at now,
I don't know what I'll do then,
without both of you by my side

For, now I'm clutching on to his,
 holding him tight
Afraid to watch him wither away,
like I watched you that day...

40. I Held On Too Tight

Everything I love,
I hold it too tight
Enough for it to break,
without a fight

Like those shoes, I never wore to keep them safe,
 slowly with time withered away,
The rose I kept safe, rotted all its days away

Everything I love I hold it too tight,
I question my intentions staying up at night
Do I clutch to hard, they yearn for freedom?
Or maybe they just do it out of spite

41. The Timing Wasn't Right

I'm not the type people want as a wife,
I'm the type whose timing just wasn't right

Too early, too late,
it was all just a mistake
I'm never the one,
 I'm the one they find before it

After me,
the next one, that's it
Just their type,
 I guess my timing,
Just wasn't right

42. Other Grandparent's Home

In the other grandparents home,
There lay a photo display,
Showcasing their kids, grandkids,
all in one way, the perfect family

All except one was there,
 the one who felt like the spare,
Since the minute she breathed that first breath of air,
She knew she was second, would come below,
no matter how hard she could never glow,
could never shine harder,
what's the point right?
After all, the stars don't shine brighter
than the moon at night

Each time she'd visit she'd see the photo frames,
wondering why one never showed her face,
she was happy at the sidelines, cheering for the others,
 the clearly superior kids

But as the years passed on, she stopped staring at the photo
frames,
 stopped wondering why one never bore her name
When after years the grandparents asked,
if they could put a frame with her face, she softly chuckled
and said
'what a shame, for now I don't long for it'

She slowly stopped wishing to fit in,
she found herself enough,
easing away her pain...

43. The golden child

Families are suppose to be gentle and kind,
then where did mine go wrong?

Why was my childhood, just a bed of thorns?
The constant comparisons with my brother,
He's smarter, he's wiser, he is better

Everyone around me,
clearly didn't want me there,
 so slowly I stopped trying,

I watched the spark in me fade,
That one dinner, was all it took
For me to realise, that I was far better,
 alone with a book

With every comment they passed,
Every tear I held back, I understood,
They only see the things I lack,
Maybe it wasn't gender biased,
Maybe my brother was it for them,
the golden child

I've somewhat made peace with it,
 and maybe soon I'll be alright

44. The glass child

The glass child, the overlooked ones,
I was just there, but was never the one

The one they talked about,
the one who did something,
something they could brag about

I was the one who couldn't have a hobby,
for the year I learned piano,
I was just too late

My sister learned it first, won their hearts,
the year I learned to sing,
My sister became a prodigy with the voice of a star

I was an introvert but I couldn't even have that,
for I'd constantly get told,
your sister's double the introvert that you are
but she still tries, still sings the songs,
why don't you ever try

So I stopped learning piano,
I stopped singing songs
For I stopped doing everything I knew she did,
 even if it was wrong

Letting the things that made me happy, all slowly slip
But nobody notices, nobody cares,
I'm the glass child, the odd one out of my kin

45. I Wish I was Home

I wish I was home,
even though I am
I wish home was a place of warmth,
Of comfort, affability,
but mine is of corpses, of who I once was

The person that died, but still lives
I have air in my lungs but no will
I'm only just surviving I'm not living
For to live I'd be happy,
not on the verge of dying

I wish I was home,
for this place isn't it
This isn't what I remember,
from the days I wanted to live
Home isn't a safe place for my mind anymore,
but I still wish, I was home

46. The Missing Piece

The missing puzzle piece when will she find hers?
The one that was broken off her
 when she was just a wee little girl

The one most important piece of her heart,
 the one she'd never find
no matter how she searched far

For it died and burnt to ashes along with the wind,
 and the one person she knew without she couldn't live
Instead they took her missing piece

And left her with wounds,
deep ones to deal with alone,
The other family pretending to tend,
only poured salt down to slow the mend

For now she still searches for that special piece,
the one she never got,
the one that mattered most,
The one that made her life
stand still at a hold....

47. Over A Bad Grade

Most girls my age,
Well they cry of heartbreak,
That is when they're heart shatters
and crumbles

I cry alone, in my bed
Not because of a boy
But because of this brain
The knowledge it can't retain
I cry because of a bad grade

Each time I see anything less than an A
 my heart breaks, my head hurts
and I waste another day, because what's the point?
No matter how much I try I'll never be what I was,
everything I had didn't stay

I crumple my test in my hand,
and throw it away, it's not what I planned
Then I crawl back into my comfort place,
and waste the day, crying over a bad grade

48. Happier Instead

Maybe in another life
I loved my school,
I had friends, the teachers were good

Maybe in another life,
I'd have been the perfect child,
instead of the one, they often forget

Maybe in another life,
 I wouldn't wish to be dead
Maybe, in that other life,
I'd have been happier instead

49. The Language Of The Eyes

The language of the eyes,
To know it is a gift,
Being able to say so much,
in just a ricochet

The language that has no deceit,
To find someone to use it with,
that's such a feat

For in the world of texts and voice calls,
the language of the eye,
it seems rather lost

50. To Write A Letter And Send It Off

To write a simple letter,
and send it off, is a dying cause
Simply to friends, family
or maybe a lover

Writing a letter is truly like no other
For the smell of ink,
the smell of words,
pure thoughts on paper,
brings quite the pleasure

If only I had someone to write a letter to,
 well then it wouldn't be sad,
for I have no friends, no family
and definitely no lover

To write a simple letter
 and send it off,
to places unknown is a wish set in stone....

51. Your Eyes and Mine

I look in your eyes
and see the ocean,
You look in mine
and see darkness

If only mine were lighter too,
Maybe they'd be more beautiful
Like you

If only you could drown in mine
 like I do in yours,
 every time I stare
just a second too long

52. Scars

The scars on my arm are a reminder,
Of the way I felt,
why I wanted it to end

I hide them away
like they bring me shame,
They take me back to the time
when I cut my arm,
because I hated my name

I hated how they made fun of it,
Like my name wasn't normal,
 like it was a thing to laugh at

I wanted a whiter name,
I wanted to change it,
but when I finally decided to it all felt wrong,
for who would I be if my name,
wasn't the one used in that one song

That one song you used to like,
so I learned all the words,
the one you'd play sitting under the stars at night

53. I Notice The Little Things

I notice the little things,
The way you look around nervously,
The way you play with your fingers

I notice how you walk a little slower with me,
 to help me enjoy the little things,
unaware that when it comes to little things,
I may not know much

But when it came to little things about you
I could identify without a touch,
your different kinds of laughs,
the little eye rolls you do,

The way you groove,
listening to that rapper dude,
I don't even like him but for you,
I'd listen to it for hours straight

For you,
 I'd be the first in line to buy concert tickets of his,
 they're not worth it you say,
but I see that glint in your eyes,
even for just a little bit,
For I notice, the little things

54. I Hate Men

I hate men,
The way they stare,
the way,
well they don't even care

They'll only like you
if your under a certain weight,
decorate their arm,
to speak hesitate

The girls alone at night
are always afraid, not all men they say
But always a man, neigh?

For if men didn't exist,
we wouldn't have to care,
about the length of our skirt,
 the neckline of our shirts, our waist
To give our all, only for it to end
and be called two faced

55. The Roses Smell Like Poison

The roses smell like poison,
Like a sickening sermon,
their scent plays
and messes with the workings of my brain

Your no good,
but the poison makes it sweet,
enough to slowly choke me,
 till I can't breathe

The roses smell like arsenic,
Like a bitter old tonic,
They burn my throat and lungs
But I let them do so with pleasure,
For I'm not sure why,
but I seem to enjoy the burn

56. Maybe On Venus Or The Sun

I wish for a miracle,
Up in the stars, take me away,
To a planet, maybe mars

The winter nights far too cold,
the summers too warm,
I want someone to remember me,
when they hear that song

The one the singer wrote,
about his college sweetheart,
 like the painting the sick artist made,
of the nurse he loved,
 maybe I might experience that love too,
probably not here, but maybe Venus, or the sun

57. A Life Of Woes

The stars they never meet,
the sun to the moon, never shows
What a sad little life full of woes

I wish for a merrier end,
than that of the cosmos,
to be born and end both with a bang
That is a sad little life full of woes

To die alone, would be far better
than to die knowing I've loved and lost
For the regret, would forever blow
That is a sad little life full of woes

58. Write A Guide To Murder

Write a guide to a murder,
That's my life's goal,
the perfect plan, to take control

To take control over my life,
my mind and everything I know
Make it my life's goal

Heal my trauma, maybe one day fine
Maybe I'll have someone to call mine,
as the sun sets and the nights show
That is my life's goal

59. Pink

Pink, why'd they deem it girly?
For that tinge of pink on your cheeks,
 when you blush is the world's most beautiful thing

On you my dear, it looks most masculine,
it makes me want to be the cause,
makes me want to take a pause
and look at your charming face

If only that could be the case,
Why'd they deem pink girly?
It's certainly not,
when it fills the tops of your ears,
seeing it all my tears, they simply go away

I don't know why they said pink's for girls,
since on you darling,
it looks like the most marvellous thing

60. Being A man

Being a man might just be
the world's most wonderful thing,
Not having to be scared,
walking alone at night

Not looking over your shoulder,
estimating when,
that creepy stranger will bite

Not all men they say, but it's always one,
The girls need to know better,
 it's been said since the tale's begun

Being a man might as well be,
getting a head start, fifty meters ahead
Then the rest of the others forced to play with dolls,
forced to act small

61. Time Heals, But Mine Doesn't

They say time heals all,
But mine mocks me,
Taunts me how I waste it away

I know I do, but I just can't stop,
Can't get out of my comfort zone,
Can't drop that ball

They say time cures,
But mine breaks me down,
beats me into a million pieces
Makes me feel like a clown

They say time heals all,
but is it really true?
For when I look at the clock,
it makes me feel blue

62. Oh To Be Skinny

I wish I was skinnier,
Everyone tells me I should be
How if only I was lighter,
I'd be so pretty

You'd be the prettiest girl,
if your thighs weren't fat,
if your cheeks weren't chubby,
if you weren't so plump

They make jokes at the family gatherings,
about how much I eat,
I used to try to defend myself,
but I know they can't be beat

They won't shut up, they won't stop
After all, what else would they joke about?
 If not for the lunch I had,
so at dinner, I pretended I wasn't hungry

Went to bed with pooling eyes,
felt so angry, so meaningless
Just wishing to be smaller

63. Not Exist At All

I wanna leave,
I've stressed this enough
But not just my home
My body, my soul

I wanna leave,
Not exist at all,
Maybe one day I will

But that day seems far
If only I had the courage
to draw that scar

64. The Thought Of Love

I fell in love, with the thought of love
I wanted to experience it,
But I don't think I ever will

I'd be the depressed writer,
sitting home alone, paying bills
The thought of love excites me

Adrenaline rushes through,
But then the fear takes over,
What if the one I experience isn't true?

So I give up, and learn to be
In love, with just the thought of love

65. The Middle Child's Miseries

The oldest, the pride
The youngest, the joy
The middles?

Well, they're rather coy
And used to being forgotten
To not being the ones spoiled rotten

The youngest, get whatever the want,
the oldest?
Well they can do no wrong

The middle child, neither right nor wrong,
to feel loved, they try but eventually
come undone

They lie and tell themselves they'll be okay,
Maybe it'll all get better with age

66. The World's Most Dangerous Thing

The most dangerous thing in this world is to love,
For your heart must eventually get shattered
or lost, forgotten and tattered

It's the riskiest to know more about someone else,
than you do about yourself
The silliest to watch, whatever they do,
 to help them get that book from the high shelf

To love, is the most dangerous thing in this world,
For you must give and give,
never expect return

67. Hope Of Us

The time ticks,
It's slipping away
Everything I try,
it fades away

The memory, of every fold of your face,
 it's going away trace by trace
You've moved on,
I know you have

But my love,
I've stayed in the past,
Trying to stop time,
when it was good,
 I'd stay in that moment
for forever if I could

The moment I knew your reactions by heart,
all the childhood stories of your scars,
the scars I loved to trace along, while you hummed
and sang your favourite song

The ticking clock brings me back,
From the past, of what I cannot have
I try, and try but it all fails,
The hope of us, it's fading away

68. The Town Whose Name Sounds Like A French Perfume

Up over the mountains
 is where I wanna live,
In that little town,
whose name sounds like a French perfume

Where each winter,
the snow blooms,
where the world is most still
up over the mountains, is where that is

The little town life,
the little town markets,
that's how I want to live
In a little town where,
on cold morning white fog looms,
The little town, whose name
sounds like a French perfume

69. If I Didn't Try

Maybe if I didn't try to do it all,
I'd be better at something
Wouldn't feel so dang small

Maybe if I had the courage,
maybe I'd be able to talk,
to large crowds
And not feel insignificant

Maybe I'd be the leader
 I dreamt to be, maybe I'll be one
even after I wake up from my dreams

So maybe, if I didn't try to do it all,
I'd be better at something,
Wouldn't feel so dang small

70. I'm Left Alone

At the end of the day, I'm left alone
Maybe it'd be better, if I sold my soul
For who do I confide in,
 for comfort, for warmth

I'm simply all alone,
with that old shirt I took of yours,
 I still smell your cologne,
 without you this house, it isn't a home

Since you left, I'm all alone
All that's left of me now,
 Is just skin and bones
At the end of the day, I'm left alone

71. Down A Stream

No matter how hard I try,
I don't fit in,
Like I used to, just blend in
No longer the one people wanted to be

The one they'd want to study like,
I had so many ideas at a young age
Of what I'd do when I am, the age now
But now, I know nothing,
nothing, to separate me from the crowd

What am I even doing now,
With my life, my hopes and dreams
Floating away slowly,
Slipping away down a stream

72. Glass And Gold

The glass child is what I am,
They look right through me.
The older one, that's more important
The golden child, be more like him

I grew up, tearing away every shred of who I was
 to be just like him.
I tried to paint my glass gold,
but it was still just glass, after all
I ripped my personality away,
My interests, my hobbies, I let it all decay

I read the books he read,
tried to lead the life he led,
But that still wasn't enough,
because no matter how shiny,
Glass will always be worth less than gold, after all

73. The Best Friend I Don't Talk To Anymore

The song, my best friend I don't talk to anymore
listened to, plays as I drive down the road
It's become my favourite, something about it
feels familiar, feels warm

We don't talk anymore, but her broken pieces,
are still in my hands, and mine in hers
We fixed ourselves with them
You could say we're now interconnected forever,
no matter how far we go,
no matter how long it's been since we last spoke

When that song plays, the other will always find it familiar,
the feeling of warmth, for we complete each other
even if we aren't together

74. Me By My Side

People say I'm a nice person,
 but I don't believe them
There's a person inside me,
 I wish, I could push away

But they're the one who comfort me,
when I'm crying late at night
The one I turn to at the end of the day
Sure, they'd burn the world,
but me? they'd hold tight

They wipe my tears and say times will get better
They close me off from the cold cruel world,
 and protect that little girl, I used to be

That's everything most girls want in a guy,
but I have it inside me,
and I know I'll be alright, if I have me
By my side

75. A Poet's Epiphany

To write a poem is somehow,
The worlds easiest yet most arduous thing to do,
for people say to simply write rhyming words,
but, where do I get a clue?
About the words to describe
the frail, lovesick human mind,

For how do I describe how the heart once broken,
bleeds but still beats hopelessly,
 in hope of being mended again

They ask why I love poems,
why all the time writing I spend?
Finding the right words to describe the little things
 The smell of her hair, how it was his favourite scent
How waiting for him, decades she spent

A poem is described as a short verse with a rhyme,
Ask a poet you see, it's a way to travel back in time
Back to when, the days of old, were new
Back to the smell of fresh coffee, my father would brew,
While mother made the pancakes and sang whatever song,

To write a poem is somehow,
The worlds easiest yet most arduous thing to do,
for people say to simply write rhyming words,
 but where do I get a clue?

76. I'm Rude

They say I'm rude and sure,
Maybe that's true
But how do I explain it to them?
The feeling within, that makes me want to be alone
It's a call deep from my soul,
I breathe most comfortably, when I'm with me

For alone, it's easy to be
I don't need to question every action I do
No matter how close I am with people,
I'm closer with myself

For it's just easy to be with one's own mind

77. To God

If I could, I would
Write a letter to god
Make all my miseries go away

But then what would be the fun, of waking up the next day?
What would I have to look forward to, or to dread

For if I made god take away my miseries,
 I'd be further miserable instead
The twisted joy I get from them, it'll be gone

What would I do without a life like mine, that's flawed
So maybe, just yet
 I won't write that letter to god

78. 1,850 days ago

We haven't talked in almost a month,
20 days ago, we said we'd be in touch
but I guess it was all for show

You've got new friends, I'm leaving this town
Only 94 days, I'm around,
And then we'll be strangers, like we were

 that day we first met,
1,850 days ago
When I walked in that classroom

Funny to think, how we lost contact
When I didn't text first, since you forgot to text back

Maybe I didn't see it then,
maybe this was already dead, months ago
but I kept its corpse, preserved for as long as I could

Woefully now, the decay
It's starting to show

79. Atlantic's Secrets

The Atlantic it's deep,
Hides secrets within
Like how I hide mine,
When I look at your face

I watch from afar,
I wouldn't dare come near
Seeing me, you'd lose all that cheer

I wish I could tell you how, I love your sight,
Your chocolate brown hair,
how it glimmers golden in the light,
The way you tap your feet sitting in class

I'd write Letters upon letters to you,
If I had the chance
 for now, you'll never know
at least not in this life

But maybe in the next one,
 the idea of us, won't give me such a fright

80. Every Winter With You

I like winter better, it's the season
Of comfort, of hope
Summer's okay but winter's winter after all

It's the reason I tell people,
But in truth I fell in love with winter
Because of you,
The smell of your sweaters,
drinking hot chocolate with you

That little cafe up on the block,
Where we'd go, fill up on eggnog
It's not the season I like, it's the time
I spent with you

I wish I could've spent
every winter with you

81. Little Miss perfect

The artist I used to listen to,
I say I hate her now
Cause that's all she listens to

Little miss perfect,
The stories she posts,
about her friends, that party, her whole life
Makes me wish it was mine

I say I hate her, hate her life
But maybe I'm just a bit jealous inside
It's cause I know I'll never be like her

I know it sounds pathetic,
And maybe that's all that it is
Maybe one day, I'll be fine
Knowing I'm not miss perfect

I'm just myself and that's all right

82. I'm Glad To Leave

Now that I'm leaving,
The fake pleasantries come,
"We'll miss you" they say
But I know, they'd never care anyway

They'd never invite me,
To birthdays, parties, or even to sit with at lunch
Never want to talk to me,
Always so stuck up

I'd hate leaving,
But maybe it's what's best for me now,
 start afresh,
leave all this behind

I'm glad to leave,
before I ran out of time

83. "Was Any Of It Even Real?"

Was any of it real?
Was it all just a dream?
Was I just stuck between the parallels of reality?

The woven stitches of time, they've ripped
I couldn't distinguish reality, the dreams
I gnawed at the seams,
Worsening the tear, I hate it here

This isn't the place I thought it was,
The stars aren't aligned,
No, it was never a sign

And then, I wake up,
Flustered and stunned,
What did I just see? What was it?
The thought, well above my mind
And all that's left is for me to ask

"Was any of it even real?"

84. I Wish I Could, But I Don't Have It In Me

I wish I looked better, lighter
Wish I had it in me, to burn in the fire
Wish I could be cold enough to myself

Wish I could make my body starve,
Help it look better,
It's what everyone says, "just cut out the carbs"

But I can't, I know once I do
There's no return
I'll sit in the bathroom watching my body burn,
First the calories, then my skin

It'll hollow me out, slowly from within
I wish I looked lighter but is it worth it to be?
 if it shatters my soul,
Makes it hard to breathe

85. Pick And Choose

Would it be easier?
If I don't leave now,
 If I stay another day
Would it make it easier?

I've never spent life away from you,
I physically don't know what it's like
If I could you'd be the first thing
 I pack in that suitcase of mine

So would it be easier, when I'm older?
 Everybody seems to think so.
Everybody but you

My mind, craves the freedom
But misses the warmth,
Why can't I have both? Why must I pick
and chose what I find dear most?

86. I'm Not Edgar Allen Poe

"It'll always will be you"
It's the phrase I told god about,
The one I whisper to myself
To try to lighten the self doubt

I cry in my bed
 turn of the light, and try to sleep
But my mind, it races away deep
I don't know, how to think, how to be

I'm not Edgar Allen Poe, for me the moon never beams,
doesn't bring me dreams of my Annabelle Lee
For me my Annabelle, he doesn't even know I exist

Even if he did, I doubt he'd think what I think, I'm not his
type
He wouldn't want to stay up late, gazing stars at night

So everyday, I tell myself it's alright,
After the days done and I've cried
I read Annabelle Lee, to give myself hope

Maybe one day, I'll hear the phrase
I tell myself most
"It always will be you"

87. I Hope

I hope your happy,
I hope your smile makes someone's day brighten
Like it used to mine,
I haven't seen it in a while

Not since the last we talked,
Been a while, since I took that walk, down memory lane
So here we are again

I hope your glad,
I hope your now okay with your dad,
about that stupid fight you had
I hope you put your differences aside
I hope you hugged each other tight
I hope you got if off your chest,
Held his embrace and cried.
Cried it all out, I hope you're feeling better now

I hope nothing changes about you,
I hope you learn to live, and love yourself again
I just hope your not afraid, to be happy again

88. I Felt Bad But Now I Don't

I felt bad leaving but now I don't
Now those two months I dreaded,
Can't come soon enough

I just want to leave, get away from all this
I thought at least you were with me but turns out you
weren't

And all that took for me to see, was for him to come back
Now suddenly I'm irritating, I'm annoying and he's taken my
place

And all he needed, was to just come back from college,

Looking back it was so naive, so foolish of me to think
 that I could ever be the favourite child,
 or just even liked

89. Second Thoughts

You died when I was too young
 to remember most of the time
 I spent with you, I thought I'd be,
I was your favourite

But now, I'm having second thoughts,
maybe I won't be above him, to anyone after all

Maybe I made you up to feel wanted,
 to feel like I was, at some point in my life

But now, I'm having second thoughts....

90. Tried And Got The Guy

Maybe in another life
Maybe in another time
You could've been mine

Maybe I would've had the courage,
To talk to you, to let you know I exist
Maybe I would've been your 'type'
But not this time,

Maybe in an alternate universe,
I'd have been fine, knowing
I tried and got the guy

91. Me, Myself We Cry

The only person
who ever truly loved me is me,
the one who'd chose me first

It sounds selfish, maybe narcissistic too,
but trust me if you felt nobody wanted you, loved you,
would chose you,
well then maybe you'd get a clue

Call me a brat, anti social, selfish, a narcissist,
but I was the one who held me when I cried,
I was the one who wiped my tears
while they gave them to me

So just let me be, I'm fine,
 perfectly happy in my own company
I'm the only person I feel at home with,
 I feel comfort with,

They raised him well,
made me raise myself,
but I was just a child too...

92. What I Long To Be

The poet, is what
my poor melancholic soul is,
The king, my heart wants to be,
The soldier, what I should be,
The fighter I was never born to be

I don't want this kingdom,
Which wasn't even meant for me
I must pertain, to this palace of agony
For it's in my blood's, twisted symphony

They can be the kings, the ministers,
The soldiers, as much as they please
Let me be the poet I long to be

Just let me be the poet I long to be

93. In A Paris Café

I wish I could take my troubles away,
And write a poem on a warm afternoon,
In a Paris Café

I wish I'd had the chance,
Run away, to little old France
I'd paint its flag, blue from the
Ice in my veins, red from the blood
Once thawed and white from the empty page

Waiting to be filled, sitting in a Paris Café

94. Those Old Bollywood Songs

Old Bollywood songs,
They understand me like no other
Where did we go wrong?
Can't we just go back? To those old songs

As a kid, I'd ask my parents to turn off
Those old depressing tunes, but now
There's nothing I relate to more

They make me feel not alone,
In the mess of it all
Its sounds so cliché,
like, those songs
But somewhere along the road,
We went wrong, I just want to return
To those old songs

95. I See You In Her

I hated mirrors,
I hated what they showed
But maybe now, I like what I see
For there's a little bit of you in me

I only remember you from that photo,
You in a blue dress, with a resting face
Of agony, just like mine
I see a little bit of you in me

Genetically I'm you, about twenty-five
 percent, but I can't remember the time
We spent, they tell me we were
Inseparable but, bitter time separated us

For now,
You're nothing more than a picture
You aren't here but you
made me love her, the person I see
In the mirror, for I see a little bit
Of you in her

96. The Bitter Kind Of Happiness

The bitter kind of happiness,
The sweet kind of sadness
Ironic but irrevocably what describes
It best

Bitter out of situations,
Happy to be leaving them,
Sweet were the little glimpses
Before sadness crept over them

The bitter kind of happiness,
I wish upon none,
The sweet kind of sadness
The selfless ones feel

Ironic they are, rather oxymoronic
But irrevocably what describes
That feeling best

97. You're Not Depressed

'You're not depressed', they laugh
How could you, your barely fifteen
You have a roof over your head,

You have nothing to worry about,
But what about the thoughts in my head?
The ones telling me, my body is ghastly
The ones who make disgusted remarks
At the marks, on my face?

'You're just a kid', I wish but I'm not
I see girls my age, and then look at my scars
I don't have the waist, the stomach,
the skin, the complexion

I'm not scared of others, but of my own rejection
 The rejection of those voices in my head
For it's from them, I crave validation more
Than anyone else

98. Like It's My Poison

I tell people I love coffee,
I drink it alone like
It's my poison

I sit in my room,
Trying to write, the artist in me
Trying to survive, for it's in the nightmares
Of my nightmares that I see

The artist in me dying,
Dying of obscurity and fading in
The sea of unnoticed art,
That came before me

I do not wish for fame,
But to live for my art
Those words on a page
That speak to my heart

All these thoughts cloud my brain,
While I sit in front of an empty paper
That's calling my name,

I pick up my poison,
And take a sip,
Hoping this time it'll hit, and break this wall
Of writers block

99. Tear Stained Pillows

Maybe in the end it'll be worth it
Every breakdown, every tear I shed
Maybe I'll be okay in the end

But I'm not right now, and I can only live
With the hope that I soon will be,
In the end, I'll be okay

Maybe in the end
I won't cry, staining my
pillows of tears everyday
And maybe it'll all be worth
Even though, I know its quite cliché

100. The Stages Of Grief

The stages of grief are five,
But I've been stuck in the fourth one
For a while,

Depression, it's what stroked me at night
While I sit in my room,
Alone with a smile and tears running down
My face, I try to bargain

Maybe if I end it all? I'd be happier?
Then anger within me takes place,
Why couldn't I have just been better,
'Enough'?

As the sun rises, denial comes in play
"I'm okay", I tell people, lying to
myself through the day,
The final stage, acceptance never comes,
For I simply can't accept that I will never
Be enough.

I simply can't accept that I will never be
enough.

101. Goodbye

Goodbye old friend, this is it
The end.
The two words, so short so simple
But take so much effort to say

For now, we'll never meet again
Maybe someday, but never like this
Goodbye old friend,

I hope one day I'll see you again
and this time, time will be on our side
There'll be no tears, no goodbyes

But for now the clock is against us,
I must go, we didn't get much time
But maybe one day, you'll be mine, again

Till then, goodbye old friend

Farewell, sweet friend